FAMOUS PEOPLE
FAMOUS LIVES

Biographies of famous people to
support the curriculum.

Diana,

Princess of Wales

by Harriet Castor

Illustrations by Hemesh Alles

W

FRANKLIN WATTS

NEW YORK•LONDON•SYDNEY

First published in 1998 by
Franklin Watts
96 Leonard Street
London
EC2A 4RH

Franklin Watts Australia
14 Mars Road
Lane Cove
NSW 2066

ISBN: 0 7496 3281 X

A CIP catalogue record for this book
is available from the British Library.

Editor: Kyla Barber

Printed in Great Britain

Diana, Princess of Wales

Diana was born on 1st July, 1961. Her parents, Johnnie and Frances Spencer, already had two daughters and had been hoping for a boy.

Johnnie needed a son because, when his own father died, he was going to become Earl Spencer. He wanted his son to be the next Earl Spencer after him.

So Johnnie and Frances had another baby after Diana. This time it was a boy. They named him Charles.

But Johnnie and Frances weren't happy together. When Diana was six years old, they got divorced. Diana and her sisters and brother were very sad.

Diana's grandfather died and
Johnnie became Earl Spencer.
He and the children moved to a
big house called Althorp. It was
so big that it wasn't cosy.
The children didn't like it.

8

Diana, like her brother and sisters, was sent away to boarding school. She had lots of friends there. She liked looking after her pet guinea pig, and swimming, and she loved ballet lessons.

She wanted to become a ballet dancer, but she grew too tall.

For many years, Diana's family had been friends with the Queen and the rest of the royal family.

When Diana was sixteen, she came home one weekend from school. There were several guests at Althorp. One of them was the Queen's eldest son, Prince Charles. Diana was introduced to him when they were out shooting.

For her eighteenth birthday,
Diana's parents bought her a flat
in London. She moved in with
three girlfriends. Diana worked as
a teacher at a kindergarten, and
looked after a little boy for an
American family.
She loved
working with
children.

Then, when she was nineteen, Diana met Prince Charles again when she went to spend a weekend with some friends.

Diana became Prince Charles's girlfriend. When the newspapers found out, reporters started following her everywhere.

They waited outside her flat and took photos as she went to work.

Diana was shy. She found the
crowds of reporters rather
frightening. Her friends
helped her try to avoid them.

Soon Prince Charles asked Diana to marry him. Diana said yes. She loved Charles and was very excited, but she was scared too. She knew that her life was going to change forever.

When the engagement was announced, Diana had to move out of her flat. She stayed at the Queen Mother's house, and then at Buckingham Palace. But she kept in touch with her flatmates.

On 29th July, 1981, Charles and Diana were married in St Paul's Cathedral in London.
Thousands of people lined the streets to cheer as they went by. Many of them had slept on the pavements to keep their places.

Millions of people around the
world watched the wedding on
television.

Prince Charles's title was The
Prince of Wales. Now Diana was
his wife, she was called The
Princess of Wales.

They had two homes. In London they lived in part of Kensington Palace. They also had a big house in Gloucestershire, called Highgrove.

Charles and Diana were very busy. They visited hospitals and charities.

They met important politicians and royal families from other countries. They went to galas and dinners and balls.

Sometimes they gave speeches,
or unveiled plaques, or
planted trees.

Diana had hoped that, after the wedding, the newspapers wouldn't be so interested in her any more. But she was wrong. Everywhere she went, crowds of photographers went too, and she appeared in hundreds of newspapers and magazines. She had become one of the most famous people in the world.

Princess of style

When Diana was twenty, she had a baby. It was a boy. He was called William.

Royal babies weren't usually taken on official trips abroad. But when Diana and Charles went to Australia, they took William with them.

Two years later they had another son. His name was Henry, but they said he should be known by his nickname, Harry.

Though in the past royal children had often been taught at home, Diana thought it was very important that William and Harry should go to school with other children.

Like other parents, Diana went to school sports days. When there were mothers' races, she joined in. Sometimes she won!

Diana wanted William and Harry to have as normal a life as possible, even though they were royal. She took them to adventure parks and to the cinema. Once she took them to visit some homeless people. She wanted them to know how lucky they were.

Diana was still doing lots of charity work. Often she visited people who were very sick. She talked to them, and held their hand.

Because Diana loved ballet, she visited ballet companies too. She watched the dancers in class and at rehearsals as well as on stage.

Everywhere Diana went, people cheered. They wanted to touch her and talk to her.

But, although she met lots of people during the day, often she went home to an empty house at night. Sometimes she was lonely and sad.

Diana was sad, too, because she and Charles weren't getting on so well any more. Eventually they got divorced.

After the divorce, Diana carried on with her work. She campaigned against landmines – a type of bomb. She knew that because she was famous, people would listen to what she said.

Prince William suggested that Diana could sell some of her dresses for charity. Diana thought this was a brilliant idea.

There was an auction and it was a great success.

Photographers still followed Diana everywhere she went.

Diana didn't mind when she was on a work trip. But they often took photographs at other times too, when she was out with friends or going to the gym. Sometimes photographers chased her.

This made Diana very upset.

One night, when Diana was in Paris, she had dinner with a friend at a hotel. Photographers were waiting for them when they came out. Diana and her friend didn't want their photos taken.

Their driver drove very fast to try to get away from the photographers.

But he lost control and crashed the car. Diana, her friend and the driver were all killed.

Many people, even those who'd never met Diana, were very sad when they heard she was dead.

Flowers and gifts were left outside the royal palaces and at other places around the country. The piles grew larger and larger.

Diana's funeral was held in
Westminster Abbey in London.
All sorts of people, from pop stars
and politicians to charity
workers, were invited. Outside,
the streets were crowded with
people who wanted to pay their
last respects.

Diana was buried on a little
island in the middle of a lake
at Althorp, her
family home.

Remembering Diana

After Diana's death, a memorial fund was set up in her name. The money it raises will be shared out among the charities Diana supported.

At Althorp, her childhood home, a special museum has been built to house an exhibition about Diana's life.

William and Harry

Diana was always worried that photographers would start chasing her sons they way they chased her. But since her death the press have agreed not to take photos of William and Harry except at official photo calls. This is so that the two princes can get on with their lives at school, and at home with their father, in peace.

Some important dates in Princess Diana's lifetime

July 1st, 1961 – The Honourable Diana Frances Spencer is born.

1975 – Diana's father becomes Earl Spencer; Diana becomes Lady Diana Spencer.

November 1977 – Diana first meets Charles, Prince of Wales.

February 24th, 1981 Diana and Charles's engagement is announced.

July 29th, 1981 – Diana and Charles are married in St Paul's Cathedral in London. Diana become The Princess of Wales.

June 21st, 1982 – Diana gives birth to Prince William of Wales.

September 15th, 1984 – A second son, Prince Harry of Wales, is born.

August 1996 – Diana and Charles divorce.

August 31st, 1997 – Diana is killed in a car crash in Paris, France.